CHAPTER 1
INTRODUCTION

I enjoy using a good scrubby to clean pots and pans, and I've just discovered that more than one of my friends enjoys using a good scrubby, as well. As a result, more than one of my acquaintances received my handcrafted scrubbies as a present this past Christmas season. My other pals will be receiving some as birthday gifts from me in the future. They are simple to create, take little time, and are affordable. So, here's how I go about crocheting a scrubby.

CHAPTER 2
STEP BY STEP TO CROCHET DISH SCRUBBY

First

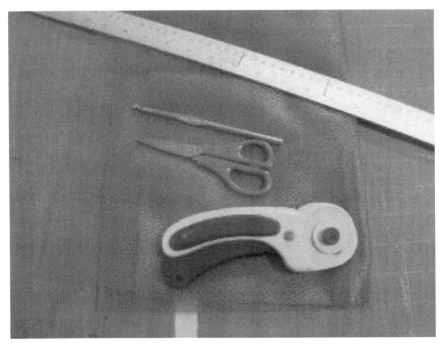

Supplies:

12 yard (.forty six meter) of internet material (plus or minus $1.00 in step with yard (.ninety two meter)) Crochet hook in length I (five.five mm) is used.

Scissors

a mat for reducing

Ruler manufactured

from metallic

Cutter using a rotary motion

Step 2:

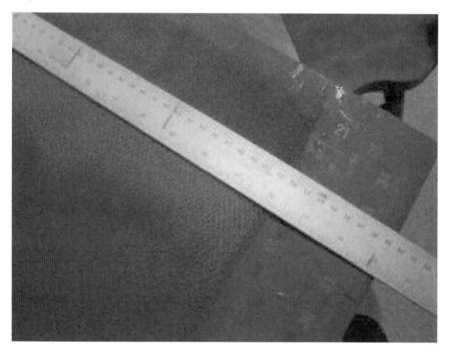

The internet material can be visible here. It is offered via way of means of the yard (withinside the United States) and is seventy two inches extensive (2 yards) lengthy. When I completed folding the internet, I placed it at the reducing mat in order that the reduce area might be inspite of the cease of the marks at the reducing mat. I located the metallic ruler at the internet, 2 inches (five cm) from the cease, and measured the gap among the 2 points.

Step three: Make a listing of all the belongings you need to do.

the use of the rotary cutter to reduce following the road that have been drawn. I reduce 9 portions of internet that had been 2 inches extensive and seventy two inches lengthy.

Step four: Make a listing of all the belongings you need to do.

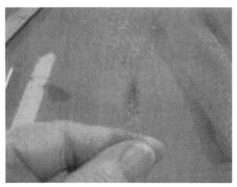

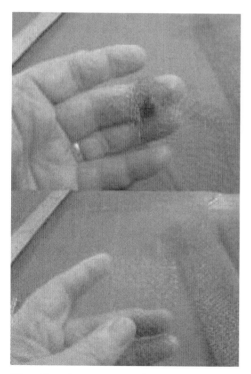

Then I took one cease of portions of internet and made them even, after which I tied a slip knot to sign up for the 2 portions collectively with a unmarried duration of string.

Step five: Make a listing of the whole thing you need to do.

Repeat the procedure with the ultimate 7 portions of internet till you've got got all 9 portions of internet knotted collectively into one lengthy duration of internet. This is the "yarn" as a way to be used for the scrubby.

Lastly, there may be a step six.

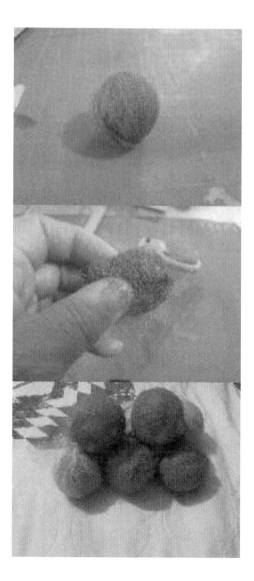

I straight away located that it's far lots superior to roll the internet "yarn" into a touch ball in place of a ball of yarn. It maintains the whole thing prepared and makes it easy to deal with.

Step 7: Make a listing of all the belongings you need to do.

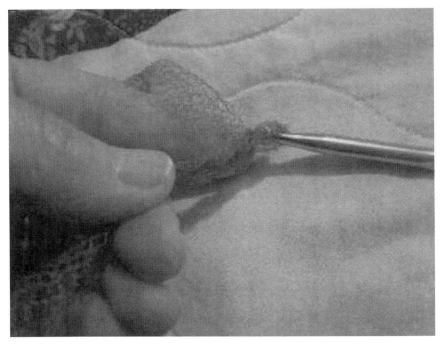

Leave a three-four inch (7.five-10cm) tail on the cease of the sew, after which chain three stitches.

Step quantity 8 is to re-compare your situation.

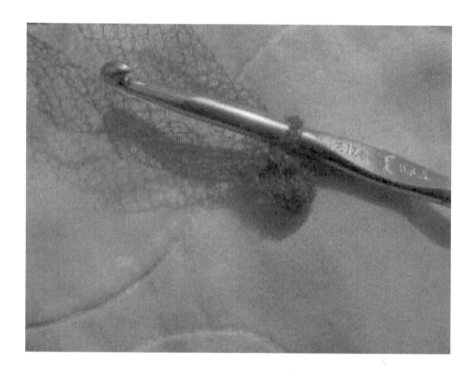

Make a tiny ring via way of means of slip sewing the second one chain

into the primary chain. Step 9: Make a listing of all the belongings you

need to do.

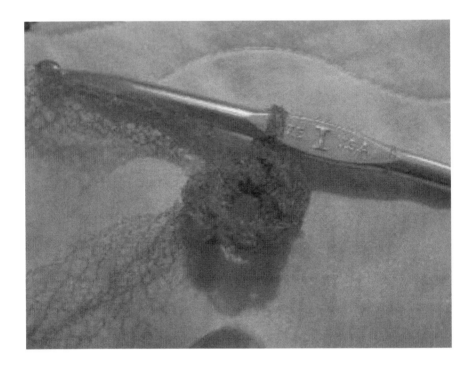

Make a sc8 into the center of the ring. You will now no longer be counting rows or rounds; instead, you'll be counting the sections of internet which are among every knot withinside the pattern. It is likewise critical to test that every knot is at the interior of the scrubby as you figure your manner thru every one. There are 9 quantities and 8 knots in all.

tenth step:

In the following round, paintings 2 sc into every sew till you attain the 2 knots (or the begin of the three strip).

eleventh step:

Once you attain the 8th knot, 1sc into every sew till you attain the cease.

After achieving this phase, you'll look at that every one of the knots are contained withinside the scrubby and that the outdoors is apparent of knots.

Step 12: Organize your information.

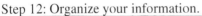

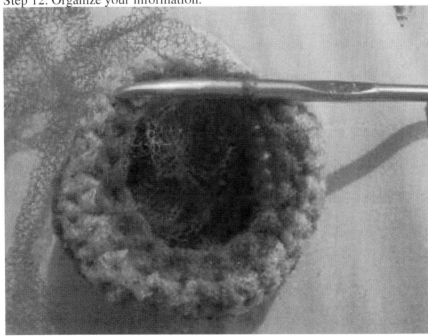

Using the very last strip of internet, you'll *sc right into a sew, bypass a sew, and sc into the following sew.

Step 13: Organize your information.

Continue till the pinnacle is absolutely closed. Tie off the closing sew as soon as you've got got completed remaining the pinnacle.

14th step:

Reach the crochet hook thru the middle hollow withinside the pinnacle, thru the middle hollow withinside the bottom, and produce the tail up thru the middle hollow withinside the pinnacle to finish the circle.

'Step 15' refers back to the 15th step of the procedure.

Tie the 2 tails collectively with a knot.

sixteenth step:

Then, the use of your crochet hook, draw the closing knot on the pinnacle of the scrubby into the center of the scrubby. It seems to be in excellent condition.

Step 17: Organize your information.

It's as easy as tossing them into the dishwasher with a load of different dishes to get them easy again. When one wears out, create any other one, or do what I do and preserve one below the sink, equipped for use as a pot scrubber whilst the time comes. Enjoy!

CHAPTER 3
HOW TO CROCHET SIMPLE DISH SCRUBBIES

After all, who desires to use an antique stale sponge whilst you may manufacture dish scrubbys? One dish scrubber may also last as long as 3 months or more!!!!!! One skein of pink coronary heart scrubby yarn yields 3 dish scrubbies (see illustration).

Supplies are the primary step.

Scrubby yarn with a pink coronary heart (one skein

makes 3) I /9-five.50mm crochet hook (length I)

Snippets of scissor

Step 2: Row 1 of the pattern

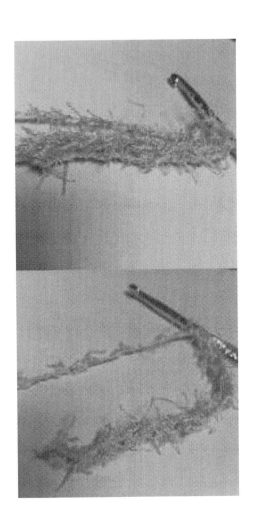

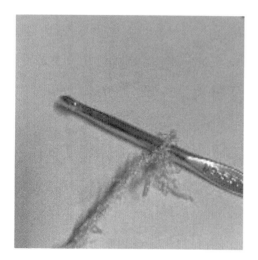

Make a slip knot and chain 15. Single crochet withinside the 2nd hook from the chain and unmarried crochet over the complete duration of the chain.

Rows 2-22 are the 1/3 step.

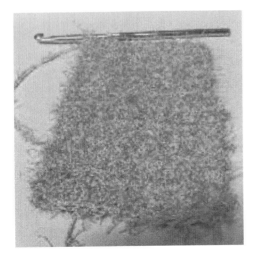

Continue to unmarried crochet in every row till you attain the cease of row 22. Not pretty completed yet, turn the piece over and sc round the rims to fasten it in place.

Tips: Put three withinside the identical hollow in every

nook of the rectangular Step four: You're completed!!!

Yay!!! You've made it all of the manner to the finish. I wish you've got got determined this manual to be useful.

THE END